# Help Me Remember the Ten Commandments

By
Delphine
Branon
Bates

I'll help you remember!

Illustrated by Delphine Branon Bates and EsDesign

LifeSong Publishers
Somis, CA

ISBN: 978-0-9799116-5-1

Copyright 2010 by LifeSong Publishers

Published by LifeSong Publishers
P.O. Box 183, Somis, CA 93066-0183
805-504-3916
www.lifesongpublishers.com

Scripture quotations are taken from the *Holy Bible*, New Living Translation, Copyright © 1996. Used by permission of Tyndale House Publishers, Inc., Wheaton, Illinois 60189. All rights reserved.

Artwork and book design by Delphine Branon Bates and EsDesign.
Printed in South Korea

**Library of Congress Cataloging-in-Publication Data**

Bates, Delphine Branon, 1945-
  Help me remember the Ten Commandments / by Delphine Branon Bates ; illustrations by Delphine Branon Bates and EsDesign.
     p. cm. -- (Help me remember series ; 3)
  ISBN 978-0-9799116-5-1 (hardcover)
  1. Ten commandments--Mnemonic devices--Juvenile literature. I. Bates, Delphine Branon, 1945- ill. II. EsDesign (Firm) III. Title.

  BV4656.B28 2010
  241.5'2--dc22

                    2010010019

# Comments

"If someone were to ask me right now, 'What did God create on the 5th day?' or 'What's the 5th commandment?' or 'What's the 5th plague brought upon by the Egyptians?'...I would know the answer! And I would have Delphine Bates and her wonderfully imaginative books to thank for it. Honestly, she has given us, young and old alike, an ingenuous way to memorize the Ten Commandments, the Seven Days of Creation and, finally, the Ten Plagues of Egypt. What's more, she makes it so easy. You really must have these little treasures in your home and church library."

—Joni Eareckson Tada, Joni and Friends International Disability Center

"With unforgettable vivid imagery, Delphine Bates creatively provides wonderfully attractive and interesting resources for aiding kids (adults, too) to indelibly etch key biblical material, like the Seven Days of Creation, the Egyptian Plagues, and the Ten Commandments, on their young minds. Every Christian parent should use these memorable materials with their children."

—Richard Mayhue, Th.D., Dean, The Master's Seminary, Sun Valley, CA

"Whether recalling a name, phone number or computer password, we often utilize word-pictures, acrostics, sound-alikes or visualization to help us remember. Amazingly, that's what the three "Help Me Remember" books do. By incorporating unique, creative and effective memory aids, Delphine Bates applies numerous mnemonic devices to tell the story of the character and purposes of God in the Bible. Refined over the years from teaching her own children and grandchildren, she now shares her secrets with us. Researched and accurately portrayed, learners of any age will find themselves easily grasping the central elements of these important parts of biblical history."

—Dr. Irv Busenitz, Vice President for Academic Administration, The Master's Seminary

To my husband, John, and our grandchildren-
JT, Curren, Whitney, Sierra, Tanner, Sheller, McKinley,
Wyatt, Ezra, Jonas, Andee, Silas, Olive, and Wilson.

"Choose today whom you will serve...
as for me and my family, we will serve the LORD."
Joshua 24:15

*Delphine*

# The Ten Commandments
(partial quotes from the following verses)

**Commandment 1:** Exodus 20:3—"Do not worship any other gods besides me."

**Commandment 2:** Exodus 20:4—"Do not make idols of any kind, whether in the shape of birds or animals or fish."

**Commandment 3:** Exodus 20:7—"Do not misuse the name of the Lord your God."

**Commandment 4:** Exodus 20:8—"Remember to observe the Sabbath day by keeping it holy."

**Commandment 5:** Exodus 20:12—"Honor your father and mother."

**Commandment 6:** Exodus 20:13— "Do not murder."

**Commandment 7:** Exodus 20:14—"Do not commit adultery."

**Commandment 8:** Exodus 20:15—"Do not steal."

**Commandment 9:** Exodus 20:16—"Do not testify falsely against your neighbor."

**Commandment 10:** Exodus 20:17—"Do not covet your neighbor's house. Do not covet your neighbor's wife, male or female servant, ox or donkey, or anything else your neighbor owns."

Be sure to read the whole story of the commandments
God gave to Moses in Exodus 20.

# The First Commandment

We must only worship the Lord God.
There is only one God!

Can you find a number 1 in this picture?

And can you find one of
anything in the picture?

*"Do not worship any other gods besides me."*
*—from Exodus 20:3—*

# The Second Commandment

Do not make any type of idol.
A swan made out of gold could become an idol.

Can you find a number 2 in this picture?

And can you find two of
anything in the picture?

*"Do not make idols of any kind, whether
in the shape of birds or animals or fish."
—from Exodus 20:4—*

# The Third Commandment

Be careful what your lips say. When you speak of the Lord God, make sure your words are honoring.

Can you find a number 3 in this picture?

And can you find three of
anything in the picture?

**"Do not misuse the name of the Lord your God."**
**—from Exodus 20:7—**

# The Fourth Commandment

The Lord God set apart the Sabbath day and blessed it. This became a special day for Him.

Can you find a number 4 in this picture?

# And can you find four of anything in the picture?

**"Remember to observe the Sabbath day by keeping it holy."**
**—from Exodus 20:8—**

# The Fifth Commandment

Honor your parents.
Look how happy this dog is when
he does what he knows he should do.

Can you find a number 5 in this picture?

And can you find five of
anything in the picture?

*"Honor your father and mother."*
**—from Exodus 20:12—**

# The Sixth Commandment

Do not intentionally
kill anyone.

Can you find a number 6
in this picture?

And can you find six of
anything in the picture?

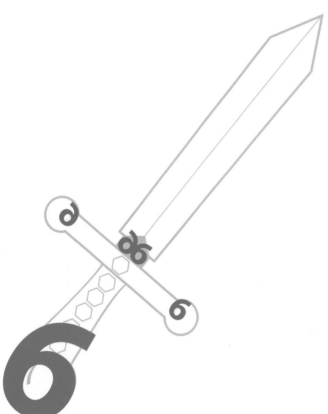

*"Do not murder."*
*—from Exodus 20:13—*

# The Seventh Commandment

Do not be unfaithful in marriage.

Can you find a number 7 in this picture?

# And can you find seven of anything in the picture?

**"Do not commit adultery."**
**—from Exodus 20:14—**

# The Eighth Commandment

We must not take what does not belong to us.

Can you find a number 8 in this picture?

# And can you find eight of anything in the picture?

## "Do not steal."
## —from Exodus 20:15—

Do not lie.
Always tell the truth.

I promise to tell the whole truth! Nothing but the truth!

Can you find a number 9 in this picture?

# And can you find nine of anything in the picture?

## "Do not testify falsely against your neighbor."
## —from Exodus 20:16—

# The Tenth Commandment

Do not covet what others have. Professional athletes make a lot of money. Do not envy what they have. Do not envy what anyone has.

Can you find a number 10 in this picture?

And can you find ten of anything in the picture?

*"Do not covet your neighbor's house. Do not covet your neighbor's wife, male or female servant, ox or donkey, or anything else your neighbor owns." —from Exodus 20:17—*

I have hidden your word in my heart,
that I might not sin against you.

—Psalm 119:11—

Thank you to everyone who has shared their ideas over the years, answered my theological questions, or cheered me on. And, most importantly, to the One who even the wind and waves obey… my Savior.

May I help you remember who He is?
John 20:31

*Delphine*

# More Help Me Remember Books

### Help Me Remember the Days of Creation
by Delphine Bates

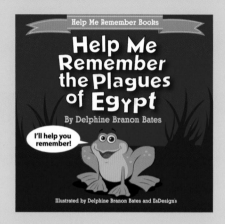

### Help Me Remember the Egyptian Plagues
by Delphine Bates

# More LifeSong Books

**Mr. Blue—A Job For You**
by Laurie Donahue and Bryan Hintz
(with cut-out pieces for puzzle and play)

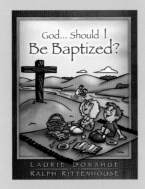

**God...Should I Be Baptized?**
by Laurie Donahue and Ralph Rittenhouse
(workbook for 8-12 years of age)

**The Lord's Supper...Let's Get Ready!**
by Laurie Donahue and Paul Phillipps
(workbook for 8-12 years of age)

Find these plus Bible Studies and
other books for adults at:
www.LifeSongPublishers.com
(or your favorite bookstore)
805-504-3916

# Ten Commandments Counting Challenge

Commandment One:    1 word, 1 number one, 1 each of the letters O, N, and E

Commandment Two:    2 wings on the swan, 2 waves in the water

Commandment Three:    3 sticks in her hair

Commandment Four:    4 fish jumping, 4 fingers on each hand, 4 lines
on the side of the boat

Commandment Five:    5 hairs on the dog's head, 5 spots on the dog's snout

Commandment Six:    6 jewels on the handle

Commandment Seven:    7 ruffles on each side of heart

Commandment Eight:    8 fingers (excluding thumbs), 8 stripes on front of his shirt
8 screws in the handcuffs

Commandment Nine:    9 curls in his hair

Commandment Ten:    10 stitches on the ball, 10 rings on the bat